MW01140170

Samuel & Comfort Alimo

Who Am I?

Daily Affirmations

Presented to

....

By

....

On

....

Never stop reciting these teachings. You must think about
them night and day so that you will faithfully do everything
written in them. Only then will you prosper and succeed.
Joshua 1:8 GW

Tips for Guardians

Dear Guardian,

This book was designed to help children know, declare, believe and express who God has made them. You may focus on a quality each day or week to let it sink deep into their minds and hearts.

- Read each affirmation aloud and have the child recite after you.
- Review the scriptures for better understanding and context.
- Ask the child for other ways they can feel or show that quality.
- Ask if the child does not yet feel or show the quality and why.
- Discuss ways to overcome any concerns and develop each quality.
- Pray together and declare the affirmations over them.
- Repeat, guide and watch them become who they really are.

I am God's masterpiece.
I am made in
God's image.
I am alive to do
good works.

Ephesians 2:10
God planned for us to do good things and to live
as he has always wanted us to live. This is why
he sent Christ to make us what we are.

READ MORE
– Genesis 1:26–28 – Psalm 139:13–14

I am loved by God.
I am chosen and accepted
in Christ Jesus.
I know His love more
through His Word and Spirit.

John 3:16

God loved the people of this world so much that he
gave his only Son, so that everyone who has faith in
him will have eternal life and never really die.

READ MORE
– Romans 8:38–39 – Ephesians 1:3–6 & 3:16–19 – Romans 5:5

I am peaceful.
I share my worries and
fears with God in prayer.
I enjoy God's peace
because I trust Him.

1 Peter 5:7
God cares for you, so turn all your worries over
to Him.

READ MORE
- Philippians 4:6-7 - Matthew 6:31-33 - John 14:27

I am joyful.
I find joy and strength in
God's promises.
I am glad because I will
see His goodness in my life.

Philippians 4:4
Always be glad because of the Lord! I will say it
again: Be glad.

READ MORE
– Psalm 119:111   – Nehemiah 8:10   – Romans 8:28

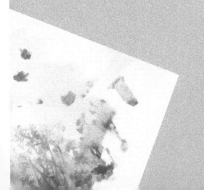

I am wise.
I have God's Word and
Spirit in me.
I choose good friends and
excel in good works.

Daniel 5:14
I was told that the gods have given you special
powers and that you are intelligent and very wise.

READ MORE
- Psalm 119:99-100   - Proverbs 13:20   - Daniel 1:19-20

I am honourable.
I honour God in
everything I do.
I respect all people, young
and old.

1 Peter 2:17
Respect everyone and show special love for God's
people. Honor God and respect the Emperor.

READ MORE
– Matthew 22:37 – Ephesians 6:1-2

I am favoured.
I stand out everywhere
I go.
I enjoy God's best for
me every day.

Luke 2:52
Jesus became wise, and he grew strong. God was
pleased with him and so were the people.

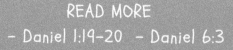

READ MORE
– Daniel 1:19-20 – Daniel 6:3

I am kind.
I am careful with my
words and actions.
I say and do what builds
me and others up.

I Thessalonians 5:14b-15
Be patient with everyone. Don't be hateful to
people, just because they are hateful to you.
Rather, be good to each other and to everyone else.

READ MORE
– Colossians 4:6 – Ephesians 4:29 & 32 – I John 3:18

I am patient.
I wait, and think, to do
what is right.
I trust God to meet my
needs on time.

Galatians 5:22-23a
God's Spirit makes us loving, happy, peaceful, patient,
kind, good, faithful, gentle, and self-controlled.

READ MORE
- Proverbs 14:29 - 1 Corinthians 13:4 - Philippians 4:19

I am faithful.
I follow Jesus fully and
use my gifts well.
I am a friend who loves
at all times.

Proverbs 18:24
Some friends don't help, but a true friend is
closer than your own family.

READ MORE
– Mark 12:30-31 – Matthew 25:14-30 – Proverbs 17:17

I am brave.
I do not fear because
God is with me.
I stand for what is right
and true.

Joshua 1:9
I've commanded you to be strong and brave. Don't
ever be afraid or discouraged! I am the Lord your
God, and I will be there to help you wherever you go.

READ MORE
– Isaiah 41:10 – Daniel 3:16–18 – 2 Timothy 1:7

I am strong.
I am thriving in my body,
soul, and spirit.
I break limitations with
God's help.

Luke 2:40
The child Jesus grew. He became strong and wise,
and God blessed him.

READ MORE
– Luke 2:52 – Psalm 18:32–36

I am creative.
I have a great mind with
brilliant ideas.
I find smart solutions
to problems.

Genesis 41:39-40a
The king told Joseph, "God is the one who has
shown you these things. No one else is as wise
as you are or knows as much as you do. I'm
putting you in charge ...

READ MORE
– Genesis 41:25-41 – 1 Kings 3 & 4 – 1 Samuel 25:2-35

I am capable.
I am able to finish what
I start.
I do my tasks well and in
good time.

Philippians 4:13
Christ gives me the strength to face anything.

READ MORE
– Philippians 1:6 – Colossians 3:23

I am a leader.
I serve God and people
with love.
I am a good example
to my peers.

I Timothy 4:12
Don't let anyone make fun of you, just because you are
young. Set an example for other followers by what you
say and do, as well as by your love, faith, and purity.

READ MORE
- John 13:12-15 - Matthew 5:16 - 1 Peter 4:10

I am a visionary.
I work towards my goals
and dreams.
I make my world a better
place.

John 9:4
As long as it is day, we must do what the one
who sent me wants me to do. When night comes,
no one can work.

READ MORE
– Jeremiah 1:5 – Philippians 3:13–14 – Jeremiah 29:11

I am a champion.
I press on to win
with God's help.
I do great things for God
and people.

Romans 8:37
In everything we have won more than a victory
because of Christ who loves us.

READ MORE
– 2 Samuel 22:36   – Hebrews 12:1-2   – Philippians 3:13-14

I am unique.
I have great value and
beauty.
I love who God has
made me to be.

Psalm 139:13-14
You are the one who put me together inside my
mother's body, and I praise you because of
the wonderful way you created me. Everything
you do is marvelous! Of this I have no doubt.

READ MORE
– Jeremiah 1:4-5 – Jeremiah 29:11 – Psalm 139:13-16

WHO AM I?
Scripture References

MASTERPIECE
- Ephesians 2:10
- Genesis 1:26-28
- Psalm 139:13-14

LOVED BY GOD
- John 3:16
- Romans 8:38-39
- Ephesians 1:3-6 & 3:16-19
- Romans 5:5

PEACEFUL
- 1 Peter 5:7
- Philippians 4:6-7
- Matthew 6:31-33
- John 14:27

JOYFUL
- Philippians 4:4
- Psalm 119:111
- Nehemiah 8:10
- Romans 8:28

WISE
- Psalm 119:99-100
- Daniel 1:19-20 & 5:14
- Proverbs 13:20

HONOURABLE
- Matthew 22:37
- Ephesians 6:1-2
- 1 Peter 2:17

FAVOURED
- Luke 2:52
- Daniel 1:19-20
- Daniel 6:3

KIND
- Ephesians 4:29 & 32
- Colossians 4:6
- 1 Thessalonians 5:14-15
- 1 John 3:18

PATIENT
- Galatians 5:22-23
- 1 Corinthians 13:4
- Proverbs 14:29
- Philippians 4:19

FAITHFUL
- Mark 12:30-31
- Proverbs 17:17 & 18:24
- Matthew 25:14-30

BRAVE
- Joshua 1:9
- Isaiah 41:10
- Daniel 3:16-18
- 2 Timothy 1:7

STRONG
- Luke 2:40
- Luke 2:52
- Psalm 18:32-36

CREATIVE
- Genesis 41:25-41
- 1 Kings 3 & 4
- 1 Samuel 25:2-35

CAPABLE
- Philippians 4:13
- Philippians 1:6
- Colossians 3:23

LEADER
- 1 Timothy 4:12
- John 13:12-15
- Matthew 5:16
- 1 Peter 4:10

VISIONARY
- John 9:4
- Jeremiah 1:5 & 29:11
- Philippians 3:13-14

CHAMPION
- Romans 8:37
- 2 Samuel 22:36
- Hebrews 12:1-2
- Philippians 3:13-14

UNIQUE
- Jeremiah 1:4-5
- Psalm 139:13-16
- Jeremiah 29:11

For
Benaiah, Isaac and Miracle

Published in Norway by Affable Media
Email: info@affablemedia.org
ISBN 978-82-94060-00-9
Epub ISBN 978-82-94060-02-3

Printed in United States